Love Letters For New Mothers

Created by Gayle Berry,
founder of Blossom & Berry

 New Generation Publishing

This book has been created from a collection of love letters written from the heart to all new mothers, from mothers across the world.

"The moment a child is born, the mother is also born. She never existed before. The woman existed, but the mother, never. A mother is something absolutely new."

-Osho

This book is dedicated to a very special new mother, Nina Roots.

Love Letters For
New Mothers

BE
> in the moment
> brave
> proud
> realistic
> playful

LET GO OF
> perfection
> 'should haves'
> guilt

KNOW
> you are not alone
> you are enough
> you are resilient
> you are strong
> it will pass
> you did it

LEARN TO
> accept
> accept help
> be guilt-free
> enjoy it

REMEMBER
> nobody knows what they are doing
> to love yourself
> to practise self love
> to learn together
> to dream big
> to count your blessings

ENJOY
>your achievements
>each and every chapter

DO
>talk
>talk, talk and talk some more
>embrace all the emotions
>keep your identity
>be yourself
>what you think is best

GIFTS TO SHARE
>a love letter back
>pay it forward
>about this book
>useful links
>notes & thoughts

Be

- in the moment
- brave
- proud
- realistic
- playful

"People who love each other fully and truly are the happiest people in the world. They may have little, they may have nothing, but they are happy people. Everything depends on how we love one another."

Mother Theresa

BE in the moment

Dear New Mother,

Being a parent is as good or as bad as the moment you are in. The warmth of a sleeping baby curled into your body, their warm breath on your face, the heat their skin generates next to yours...it is beautiful. This is a love-inducing and magical moment.

..beautiful, until the "warmth" becomes more urgent, something more physical which now requires your immediate attention. The warmth coming from a leaking nappy can switch the magic to mayhem in an instant. Your peaceful moment is replaced by whichever mood is the very opposite of peaceful. The one that is defensive (as you shield yourself from the contents of a nappy) and disgust (look what this sweet child has produced!)...but also sharp, awake and active as you jump to protect your baby from future nappy rash and from the indignity of laying in their own faeces.

You love this child and you will continue to jump to attention as and when they need you. You will take those "bad" moments on the chin because the good ones are so good. You will spend the next 18 years of their childhood, and I'm told, beyond, swinging through the emotions; pure joy, inner calm and utter pride balanced out by genuine fear, sheer worry and frustration. Buckle-up and prepare for the ride. Know that every emotion is normal and we have to have the rain to appreciate the sunshine. This ride is worth every penny.

Love Jo x

BE brave

Dear Mama,

I know that you're scared and feel that you have so much to prove and that the entire world is judging you. You hear their whispers loud and clear; how could you be so stupid to get in this state? You've messed up your life, made a terrible mistake. They've written you off as someone who will fail, someone whose life won't amount to much now. The responsibility that you carry on your young, little shoulders is weighing you down but you dare not show it. A million questions running through your head, I mean you're just a kid yourself, how can you do this? That's what they've all said.

Well, dear Mama, I'm here to tell you that you can. You see I've been where you are, fifteen and pregnant was not in the plan. I was the clued up one out of all of my friends, the one that they came to when they needed a hand. But I was young and in love and got caught up in the moment and really didn't think about the consequences.

I remember that feeling like it was yesterday, the disbelief, the tears and so much shame, and oh my God, how do I tell my mum? What would she say? But then I heard her heartbeat, so strong and full of life and something changed inside of me and I knew it would be alright.

The day that she was born, my life changed forever. When I held her in my arms and looked into her eyes... I can't describe that feeling; it felt like magic inside.

My love for her was overwhelming and right there. At that moment I knew that it was us against the world and I was going to give my everything to this little girl.

The last 23 years have been an adventure, a journey that we've travelled side by side as we've grown up together.

We've laughed and we've cried and I've made many mistakes, but wanting the best for her was always the reason behind every decision I made.

Against all of the odds and the watching eyes, we showed them we were so much more than a statistic; we gave them a surprise. She's all grown up now and has graduated from Uni and is everything that I dreamed she would be. She's a free spirit, my warrior princess and is travelling the world because there is so much of it to see.

She is my biggest achievement and I couldn't be prouder of the baby girl that burst into my life and made me a Mama!

I want to share with you some words that I hope will see you through the times when you feel scared, lonely and question everything that you do.

It's definitely not going to be easy, but be brave, be strong, believe in yourself and know that you are more than enough and all that your baby needs.
Remember that age is merely a number and out of all of the mummies in the world, your baby chose you, so let go of the fear and be the best mummy you can be!

Proud Teenage Mama

Charmaine King

BE proud

Dear New Mama-To-Be,

Whether this is your first baby or not, you're at a crossroads in your life. It has always been amazing to me that whenever a new baby has joined our family the change in dynamics has been huge, but it has instantly felt as if it was the way things were meant to be. Within minutes I couldn't remember how life had been without them.

Having a third baby was a tricky decision for us in some ways. We already had two boys, Milo and Oakley, who were twenty-two months apart at six and four years old. They were the best of friends and I was worried how another baby would change that. I also worried about how it would change their relationship with me. They were old enough to need me in a different way and I was scared that they would feel distanced from me, both emotionally and quite literally. I had been incredibly lucky with my previous pregnancies and births. Both had been straightforward easy home births - no stitches or pain relief. I had felt prepared and in control throughout. One of the most valuable pieces of advice my mum had given me before I had my first baby is that not everyone experiences that overwhelming rush of 'love at first sight' which people talk about. So, when Milo was born two weeks early (an unplanned home birth because I had been waiting for the excruciating pain that everyone talks about and had left it too late to go to the hospital), I knew not to panic when it took several hours for that rush to kick in. My immediate feeling was of relief – and I was at ease with that. I trusted that the overwhelming rush would come – and it did, in abundance.

I had been able to breastfeed without any difficulties and both babies had been well and relatively contented. I had found myself making excuses for finding it easier than I had expected and joining in when friends needed to offload about their negative experiences. I was embarrassed and reluctant to be labelled one of those "perfect mums" and I felt a tremendous guilt for being the one who had had it so easy. Don't get me wrong, there were tough times, my eldest wouldn't let us put him down for the first six months of his life and we struggled with sleep deprivation, but I had listened to so many horror stories that it had come as a pleasant surprise when I was able to manage better than I had expected.

I knew that I had been lucky, so when considering a third, I had an overwhelming feeling that I was being greedy - pushing my luck. Still, there was a yearning that I couldn't ignore. As the birth approached, those feelings didn't subside, however, I did feel prepared and supported. I chose a lovely birthing centre as we didn't feel a home birth would be suitable for our sensitive boys in the house and in December 2015 Kitt was born following a short labour and unassisted water birth. Within three hours we were back home introducing him to his adoring big brothers, trying to take in the awe in their faces as they touched him.

For a long time, I worried that I would always have that yearning for 'just one more baby', but at that moment I knew that our family was complete. We are meant to be a family of three boys and I feel utterly satisfied and blessed. Believe me, it is not always a blissful haze. Life is hectic, chaotic, full of rough play and toilet humour, but they truly adore each other, and I wouldn't change it for the world. At times when my patience is running thin, I try to remind myself how incredibly lucky we are.

So, my advice to you as a new mum, whether or not for the first time, is to be proud of yourself and your story, whatever it is. You'll be told all the horror stories, but listen to the fairytales too. Their reality doesn't have to be yours. Positivity, preparation and a true understanding of yourself can go a long way, but if you do find that things are becoming overwhelming, be proud to speak up. If you find that you're coping brilliantly and have taken the first steps into motherhood in your stride, be proud to own it. There will always be someone who can relate. Accept yourself. Your feelings are valid.

Its okay not to be okay, but it's also okay to be doing just fine.

Much love,

Sophie x

BE realistic

Dear New Mum,

What can I say? Nothing prepares you for the highs and lows of motherhood. I didn't have my first child until I was 35. It took me a while to find someone worthy of settling down with. He came with a five-year-old daughter which has been a struggle. Motherhood is hard, but step-motherhood is even harder.

My daughter was born breach, so I never felt a contraction. I felt a bit cheated by that. Other mums said count yourself lucky - they hurt. But I always felt a like I'd missed out. I had a C-section so had to spend a few days in hospital. I remember being left that first night and thinking, now what? What do I do with this little bundle - I just wept. It was the same in the car when we bought her home. I sobbed thinking - this is it. What now? I'd read all the books, but the reality is so different. For the first six months she would only fall asleep on me or my husband which was very difficult to juggle. We chose to bottle feed as I never felt comfortable breast feeding and that way we could share the feeds. Some people disapproved that I hadn't even tried but the stresses of a new born were hard enough.

The lack of sleep was hard; I've always loved my bed. So when people say sleep when baby sleeps, take notice, you'll feel so much better for it. I remember days when I was alone, baby wouldn't sleep and I was exhausted. I'd call my mum and she'd say, 'put her in the pram and get some fresh air'. It helped hugely to get out from the four walls. I didn't join any clubs or groups and have never been one for toddler groups or meeting other mums for coffee. I wish I had been. My support mechanism was my mum, my mother-in-law and my sister. When my child was hungry and milk didn't seem to be enough, my mum said to give her a bit of baby rice mixed in. But I thought it was far too early (the book said this). But it was quite clear my child was hungry and she's no worse off for the baby rice.

We can rely too much on books. Take advice from mums who've been there and done it. Are their children any worse off for the decisions they made? Go with your gut too, you know your child better than anyone. Most of all enjoy motherhood. My children, now nine and ten years old, are so independent. They very rarely need me anymore. So, enjoy the time you have with baby. Don't feel guilty about sleeping, taking a relaxing bath, taking a few hours off to just sit and have a cuppa. You deserve it. The love you feel for your child will go up and down. Sometimes you'll look at them sleeping and your heart will melt. Other days they'll drive you up the wall, crying for hours without stopping. It's okay to not like them then. It's all natural and part of the emotional rollercoaster that is motherhood.

My advice to you new mums is; don't beat yourself up - you're doing a great job. There is no such thing as a perfect mum so embrace all the lessons you learn. If you have a second child they'll benefit from your growth as a mum. Look after yourself, just as much as baby. Don't be afraid to say when you're not coping and ask for help or advice. Lastly, but most importantly, enjoy it. It really doesn't last forever. It goes all too quickly!

Xx Zita

BE playful

Dear New Mummy,

Motherhood is a rainbow-coloured experience with every emotion and feeling. Some will serve you more than others but all emotions are there to allow you to grow, expand and understand yourself and others.

So my words are simple;

First, surrender.
Forget everything you thought you knew.
Let go of control.
Trust and learn from your baby. She will be your greatest teacher.
Stop judging yourself and others.
Accept and love yourself and your baby.
Let go of fear of the future. It's completely out of your control.
Choose love now, and whenever possible.
Let go of perfection: Do the best with what you have.
Build trust through being consistent with your word and actions.
Let go of ideals; you are beautiful just the way you are.
Don't separate yourself from others through stories you tell yourself.
Connect fearlessly with your heart.
Think less. Play more.
Become a child all over again and have adventures everyday.

Trust your instincts. They are your guide. They are usually right (but it's completely okay to make mistakes too). Know that you are an inspiration for your baby and live your life authentically through your desires and passions. Be yourself from the start. It's a long time to keep pretending you are something you are not. Reinvent yourself through motherhood (I did and it's been incredible). Hold, cuddle and love your baby. This unconditional love will nourish your soul forever.

Enjoy every minute. It's not always easy but children are the most beautiful and joyous gift in all their wonderful ways.

Much love
Gayle ♡ Mummy to three amazing children and founder of Blossom & Berry

Let go of

- perfection
- 'should haves'
- guilt

"If you are a mother, take care of the child. He needs you, he cannot survive without you. You are a must. He needs food, he needs love, he needs care - but he does not need your ideology. He does not need your ideals. He does not need your beliefs. He does not need your ideals of how he should be. Only avoid ideology, ideals, goals, ends, and then care is beautiful, then care is innocent"

- Osho

LET GO of perfection

Dear New Mum,

Welcome to the wonderful world of motherhood!

I am excited for you as you have an eventful adventure ahead; the most rewarding and everlasting job you could possibly do. As in any job, you will learn as you go along. So please be kind to yourself and don't put yourself under unnecessary pressure. Start and remain open-minded, ready to take up a challenge knowing that you are not alone, because as in any job, you will need a team, as you can achieve so much more when you collaborate and share, so please, be willing to open your heart to others and to ask and accept help.

I am thrilled for you as you will have the opportunity to build a relationship with another human being from the very beginning of his life, the most fulfilling experience you could possibly encounter. As in any relationship, it will take time to develop, so please, cherish each stage and take opportunities to connect at your own pace. Try to do this by forgetting about technology and the rushes and demands of this modern world, instead, try noticing and valuing the simple and free things in life: a smile, a gaze, a hug... If there is something my son has taught me so far, it is to find the extraordinary in the ordinary. I am sure you will find that treasure too. As in any relationship, you will find differences between you. As humans, we have different ways and tastes and these mismatches make us who we are and complement each other. You will also find differences with other mums and other babies. So please be respectful of yourself, your baby and others. Try not to have a preconceived picture of your child, simply get to know your baby and celebrate his uniqueness and show off who you are to him too, as you are also unique and amazing. With others, instead of comparing or competing allow yourself to discover and to accept diversity.

I am so so happy for you as you enter this journey finding your way, incorporating this new identity into your life; an identity you will have the power to shape and surprise yourself on how much you can possibly achieve. As in any journey, you will find that things don't always turn out as planned. Please don't worry, you will master the skill of finding different routes to similar destinations and you might need to adopt "flexibility" as your middle name. Along the way, please be compassionate with yourself, we all make mistakes and we all have a chance to rectify situations and modify our choices. You are the perfect imperfection for your baby, you are enough. As in any journey, you will need some rest and food and various things to keep you going. Please, please, please (and I reiterate this as this is one of the hardest for me) don't forget about yourself. There is so much you will want to give to your baby, all your love and attention, all your energy and your time. And that is all okay, as there is something so special and indescribable about loving unconditionally. Just remember to revisit what it is that you need to refuel, to reconnect with your inner-self. If you love yourself you will love others naturally, if you look after yourself you will be the best version of yourself for you and others.

Make yourself comfortable in this wonderful world of motherhood!

With loads of love,

Sandy

LET GO of the 'should haves'

To you Mama,

In a world full of wonderful connections, at times as a new mum, it can feel like we are being bombarded with advice and images on how we should be raising our children. There is an opinion on everything from how best to feed your baby, how to wean your baby, sleep train your baby and how its bad to rock your baby! There are even those out there who tell you how much to hold your baby! Before I became a mummy, I read and read and read but nothing could really prepare me for the real deal of these truly miraculous little beings who become the centre of your universe.

The love was, and still is, unbelievable but as a new mum I felt so overwhelmed by all the information available to me and the conflicting messages that in the first six months I honestly felt completely and utterly lost. I had a beautiful, healthy, smiley baby who I loved beyond measure yet I often felt like I was doing it all wrong. She did not sleep well at night due to reflux (and by not sleeping well I mean she was often awake every 20 minutes or so). I would literally have no sleep whilst I held her in my arms cuddling her, breastfeeding her and loving her but doing this did not stop me from feeling completely utterly alone, deep in the dark of the night.

I was given all sorts of advice including the "there's nothing wrong with her, try leaving her to cry", when I knew deep down there was something going on with her and the one thing I felt completely sure of was that I always wanted to hold my baby when she needed me and I always wanted to respond to her when she was crying, which is what I did. I always wanted her to know that her mummy is there for her. My advice to you now mama - THIS IS OKAY! You know your baby better than anybody else. They are not manipulating you! Your baby's cry is how they communicate with you, they don't have words so have to speak to you in this way. Respond, respond, respond and cuddle, cuddle, cuddle! This is what our mother instinct wants us to do so don't let anybody tell you otherwise!

At the time though, despite having this stance, I could not shake the sense of not doing things "right". Before my baby girl's reflux diagnosis, I would constantly ask myself "why does my baby not sleep and everyone else's does, where am I going wrong?" I dreaded the question "is she a good baby? Does she sleep?", it felt like it compounded my feeling of failing even more. Why did everyone else seem to be getting to baby groups, looking glam, able to cook a roast dinner and posting on Instagram about it? The other mums seem to be managing so well yet there was me who could barely muster the energy to have a shower some days.

I am incredibly lucky to have family living close by, but I felt like I needed to refuse help in order to somehow prove myself, thinking "I should be able to do this on my own, everyone else manages". However, by not taking help and not looking after me as well as my baby I became more and more exhausted and run down. I started suffering from horrible anxiety and even frightening panic attacks. It was then that I realised in order to be the best I could be, I needed to also look after me! I took help when it was offered, I came off of social media for a bit and I made sure I made time for small pleasures like a short walk, lovely warm baths and eating well. My advice to you now mama - talk to people, including health professionals, if you feel you need to. Take help when it is offered and don't feel ashamed to ask for it either! There's the old saying; "it takes a village to raise a family" and it's so true! Build a tribe around you for support, be this physically or emotionally.

If you can, get out in nature, even if it's for a ten minute walk around the block, or even the garden. Breathe in the air, look around you, really try to be here in the now and don't worry about tomorrow just yet. For me, in the thick of the sleep deprivation and anxiety, the magnolia tree in my garden kept me grounded. Over the hardest months I watched and saw the leaves fall, the buds form, and the blossoms bloom. I reminded myself of how many times I had seen this tree's beautiful flowers, and I thought to myself, this time too will pass just as the seasons change, so will my baby and so will I. I still look at that magnolia tree now and feel a deep connection. To me, it represents transition, love, and living the now.

I'm a second-time mum now and have a young baby as I write this. it's been a different experience for me as I feel so much more confident in listening to my instincts. This time around I have not read a single parenting book or manual. I follow only social media pages that promote love and connection with your baby. I speak to a few close family members and friends and chat with like-minded parents for advice instead of frantically doing online searches for answers at 3am.

My parting words – Mama you are doing a great job, and you are good enough! Your baby chose you and thinks you are amazing! You are love and your baby is love. You are connected by the heart, therefore do what feels right in your heart not what you are being told you "should" do. Enjoy the precious moments you have with your baby but don't feel bad if at times you feel like you need a break for you! No matter what difficulties you may face as a new mama, just like the seasons, this too will pass. Believe in yourself!

Carly xx

LET GO of guilt

Dear Lovely New Mummy to a beautiful new life,

You may be feeling all sorts of emotions depending on when you are reading this. Having this life changing experience -both physically and emotionally- can make you feel happy, sad, elated, scared, excited, guilty, full of love; sometimes all at the same time. What a rollercoaster this new change of role can be….and that's okay.

Being prepared, I thought, was key. I had worked with children, been surrounded by children in my family, wanted children for years. But I hadn't experienced it myself and I wasn't prepared for the challenges I faced with breastfeeding, reflux, and having a baby (now three) that struggled, and still struggles, with her sleep. I wasn't prepared for ten wake ups a night for 18 months. I wasn't prepared for the overwhelming fear and anxiety that I felt when the sun went down. I wasn't prepared... and that's okay.

I wasn't prepared for how other people can make you feel. How I let other people's judgment slip inside my mind and plant a growing seed of doubt and guilt. Some people make those judgments in plain sight, some say nothing and some are only trying to help. I felt judged for struggling, judged for voicing that feeling, judged for having a baby that didn't sleep as well as others. Who was really judging me the most? Myself. I wasn't prepared for the judgments... and that's okay.

You see, it is all OKAY. Every experience you go through as a new parent is your own journey and no one else's. It is okay to struggle, it is okay to say so. We often strive for this vision of how we feel life should be; expecting a certain scenario to play out in a certain way, expecting to feel a certain way. I had this amazing, beautiful new life that I was responsible for creating, one which I didn't even think I would have the opportunity to experience due to fertility difficulties, so why SHOULD I be struggling? Why WAS I struggling? I had no RIGHT to struggle. The guilt of not living up to expectations drowned me. At times it still does. However, with each passing day this new role I have as a Mum, a role I have wanted all my life, is becoming easier to accept and experience. I am letting go of the guilt. Now a Mum to two beautiful girls, I count my blessings every day. I also get frustrated and exhausted and even lose my temper. But the smiles and joy my girls bring to me every day outweighs it all and makes it worthwhile a million times over. "Enjoy every moment?" I certainly do not…. and that is okay.

I don't have all the answers. No one ever does and they are lying if they say they do. Every day is another day to learn and develop ourselves and strengthen our bond with our babies and children. Find your village. Find those people in your lives that uplift you and make you feel listened to and accepted. Everyone is living their own reality so there is no point even comparing our journey as mothers to others. Everyone struggles at different times, in their own way… and that is okay.

Breathe in that sweet smell of your baby, that lovely new smell that encapsulates love. Hold them when they need you because you are building the foundations of the love of the future. Follow your instinct and make sure you look after yourself as much as you can. Strap yourself in… throughout this new experience of motherhood you'll more than likely get to know yourself more than you ever have done in your life! And it is ALL okay.

Becca Xx

Know

- you are not alone
- you are enough
- you are resilient
- you are strong
- it will pass
- you did it

"Motherhood: All love begins and ends there."
– Robert Browning

KNOW you are not alone (1)

Dear Mama in a new country,
anticipating a special delivery,
planning and buying, assembling and decorating,
putting together baby's new nursery.

Dear mama in a new country,
suddenly feeling lonely,
surrounded by unfamiliarity.
Mind starting to fill with worry and uncertainty.

Dear mama in a new country,
it's okay to feel dreary, weary, considerably teary
and wondering what to do with this little, tiny baby.

Dear mama in a new country,
life is not what it used to be,
plagued with doubt, uncertainty and missing family.
Life is not what it used to be.

But, dear mama in a new country,
this feeling won't last for eternity,
feel the love from your baby.
Let his love take you to infinity.

Dear mama in a new country,
just remember you are not alone,
Mama in a new country?
The best is yet to come.

Love from, a once lonely mama.

I felt the most lonely I have ever felt in my life when I was
26 years old and moved to Germany whilst six months

pregnant. I left my very rewarding neonatal nursing job, my beautiful city apartment, my family and my independence. I felt useless. Incredibly isolated. I was silenced because I couldn't speak or understand the language. I gave birth in silence. I took him home to silence. My body healing in silence. I would hold my baby boy, look at him and just listen to the sound of silence. Day in, day out, from Monday to Friday as my now husband worked and still works away during the week. Nothing had prepared me for this lonely and incredibly emotional journey I had embarked on.

Over the months and years my silence and loneliness were, ironically, the loudest my mind has ever been. I became the most creative I have ever been. I learned an array of things about myself and slowly over time, I began to integrate into the new role of mother and foreigner. I got out and about and found the British shop which sold Tetley tea and digestive biscuits (that really helped too). Slowly, I joined baby groups, a choir, I found an English speaking church, I went to a German school, got a job at the local paediatric practice, made lifelong friends and felt like I finally became a mother to our baby boy.

Dear mamas or papas who are alone, dear mamas or papas who feel alone, you have recognised this and that's the beginning. Reach out to family and friends however far they may be, Skype or video call. Search for baby or new parent groups, discuss potential solutions with your midwife/ health visitor, partner, friend or family member. Try and get out and about, focus on something that makes you feel like you, try a new hobby just for you, don't feel guilty about asking for help and know that it won't last forever.

Most importantly remember you are loved beyond measure.

Love
J ♡

KNOW you are not alone (2)

To a New Mummy

When we found out I was pregnant, we were over the moon! I could not believe that a tiny baby was growing in me and we couldn't wait to meet our little bundle of joy. Obviously there were still nine months to go and the first four of those were filled with sleeping and vomiting a lot! And each morning, as I would look in the mirror, I did wonder when my pregnancy glow would turn up (as another piece of dry skin fell in to the sink). However, nothing can beat that feeling of the tiny flutter you feel in the pit of your tummy, wondering if it is just wind or indigestion. At about four months the sickness went and I could start to eat food that was not beige in colour or shaped like a cracker and it was then that I fully embraced being pregnant, I loved seeing my bump move around as an elbow or knee stuck out; this is one of the most amazing things you will ever see.

So, as I waddled into the hospital, little green book in hand, with my lovely birth plan of a relaxing and calm water birth, I soon realised (when my legs were up in the air, and I clutched on to my husband's hand for dear life and using a few choice words) that the lovely birth plan was long gone.

After labour I was whisked off to surgery only having seen my baby for a few short moments, but finally, after what felt like an eternity, I got to see my very relieved husband and to hold my baby girl. After settling into hospital, reality kicked in and I realised that I actually had to look after this little bundle of fun, and as I watched my husband leave us at the hospital (he was not allowed to stay with us) I looked at my baby and thought, "what on earth am I meant to do? How am I going to survive the night?"

The first night is a fond memory of being covered in black poo (the baby's, not mine) which somehow involved getting the black sticky poo all over the bed, on me and on the baby. I struggled to get her to latch on and feed and felt tired and so overwhelmed by it all. I remember thinking "I can't do this".

While my husband and I got used to being new parents, tending to our baby's needs; my amazing family came to our aid. In the Asian culture it is tradition that the mother stays at home for six weeks to recover after giving birth. However this tradition is slowly being lost as more mummies shun the confinement and reject this tradition. I am forever grateful for the help and support from my mother and mother in-law who definitely made sure I was well-fed, as I could hardly walk and was just about managing to feed my baby, let alone cook for us.

Lessons I learned………

Not everything will go to plan, no matter what is written in your green book.

Take the help and support (no matter how much you want to be independent)

Asking for help - it is not a sign of weakness. I'm sure you will find a family member or friend who would love a baby cuddle, while you go and rest or take the opportunity to have a treat with a hair wash day!

You are not alone! When you're standing at a changing table at 3am changing another nappy, tears dropping on to your cheek, thinking "will I ever sleep again?" I promise you this; although the days and nights merge into one long endless week, it will get better and you will look back at those days and remember the day you bought another amazing human being into this world. You will catch yourself saying to your husband, "what did we actually do with our lives before we had our baby?" (yes, this is hard to believe, but I guarantee it will cross your mind).

Not to compare myself to other mummies- we are all on our own unique journey- embrace it, reflux and all!

LOVE the person you are, and realise the most amazing miracle of being able to be called a mummy really truly is.

NURTURE your baby and yourself as a new mummy, allowing yourself some well-earned 'me time'.

GROW - enjoy watching your baby change and grow each and every day, being amazed and proud at each milestone they achieve, see yourself change and grow as a new mummy.

Above all, take care of yourself, love yourself and be proud of the mummy you are, at times yes it will be the most hardest job of all, but my goodness it is the most rewarding job in the world!

Love Sareena

KNOW you are enough

Dear New Mother

You Are Enough. Yes, You Are Enough.

There will be times when you wonder how the Universe could have chosen you to raise this unique complex little bundle. When you struggle to feed him. When you worry about how to best put her to sleep. When you can't soothe his crying or take away this tiny little person's terrible tummy pains. You Are Enough. Just your presence. Your heartbeat. Your embrace. This is what your baby craves.

Oh my sister, my friend. There will be moments, hours, even days or weeks when you cry a river of tears wondering how you will survive. When the exhaustion is so overwhelming that you may think crazy, dark thoughts. In these times, take a deep breath. Make yourself a cup of your favourite tea. Forget all the advice, the rules, the should haves, should nots, or should be's… and just focus on your heart space, your inner knowing, your LOVE for your baby. Know that you are doing the best you can. That YOU ARE ENOUGH. That in the morning the sun will rise, the birds will sing and you will find your mama strength to go on. It is OK to feel whatever you are feeling. It is OK to want to give up. It is also OK to ask for help. To find support on those days when you feel low. Reach out to your tribe. Connect with other mothers. Find a mothers group, a massage or yoga class, a park playdate meet up, a Facebook chat for midnight mums. Keep looking until you find that feeling of solidarity, that warm heartfelt understanding that will remind you to smile and laugh again. Keep searching until you find those people, those mama warrior sisters, those who have walked this path before you and who walk along with you now. Find these special people, these angels disguised as everyday mothers, who help you to really truly remember that YOU ARE ENOUGH.

From my mama heart to yours
Mel

KNOW you are resilient

Dear New Mummy,

Nothing in the world can prepare you for what being someone's mummy really means.

For me my journey started just over 12 years ago, my relationship was new and we were young but I knew it was what I was born to do.

Due to illness I had to be induced early and unfortunately my baby's shoulders got stuck and it went from being four people in the room to 12, it was the scariest moment of my life but when my daughter was born six days early on Christmas Eve. I felt such a rush of love that nothing else mattered and for me life was perfect.

Fast forward 19 months and after a difficult pregnancy I welcomed my son into the world weighing a fabulous 10lbs but this time things weren't as easy. He couldn't breastfeed and after battling with midwives, health visitors and every parenting book I gave up and bottle fed him. Sadly, since then, his life has been an uphill battle with speech and communication problems, three operations for a cleft palate and now he has mental health issues at only ten years old.

Every day we struggle just the three of us with health, school problems and life generally kicking our butts but I've never given up, the love for my two children keeps me going.

The main thing to take away from my story is that no matter how many books you read or what advice you're given, you know your baby, protect them, love them and most importantly love yourself.

Being someone's Mummy is the most wonderful job in the world, you will be amazing ♡

Love Jessica

KNOW you are strong

Dear New Mummy

Working in an industry where both my husband and I did lots of planning and organisation, we felt we would have this baby malarkey sorted, however…

It suddenly hit me three days after I had my gorgeous son Sebastian, just how much I was unprepared for in regard to his arrival and the impact he would have to my structured life. It sounds daft saying it now, but no amount of advice like, "you won't get a wink of sleep," or "you'll need all the help you can get," would have mattered. We waited so long for him, and although we knew it would be hard, it would get better. Surely…

In reality though (she breaks into hysterical laughter), wow, was it a challenge!

My pregnancy was flawless, with the exception of some morning sickness. This gave me a sense of naivety that my labour would be also, however, the labour didn't go according to plan in any way shape or form. After my waters broke and the midwife spotted meconium (baby's stool), I had to be induced. Long story short, after having contractions for what felt like every second for over four hours, and being just 1cm dilated, I finally got to the stage where I felt ready to push - my son however was reluctant to budge (a trait that he still has to this day). After over an hour of pushing, he got stuck and then went transverse (lying sideways), so I had to have an emergency C-section. While all of this sounds horrific, in reality, once he was born, all my adrenaline had kicked in, and the energy that had drained from my body had been revitalised just by holding him in my arms.

Hours after this major surgery (I only now realise how major it was) when my wonderful husband had fallen asleep in the hardest chair known to man and it was just Sebastian and me looking at one another, I remember holding my baby boy, feeling incredibly proud at what I had achieved in those hours prior, and how I could take on the world. What people don't tell you is how quickly this feeling can subside and how normal this is.

Reverting back to those three days after his birth, and the weeks that followed, although I had been visited by family members and close friends, and my husband on hand to help me for a couple of weeks of paternity leave, once the initial excitement of a new baby had disappeared, so did the people.

This was no fault of theirs' as I realise now that I had put myself in a situation where I had shut myself off, given myself a martyr complex and absorbed stupid remarks given to me in the early stages of motherhood. If I'm fortunate to have another child, I won't repeat this.

Unfortunately we cannot choose our family and one particular member of mine, within minutes of seeing me, actually made some frankly disgusting and idiotic comments ranging from why was I lying in bed, to trying to discourage me from breastfeeding. But the comment that stuck with me to this day (my son is almost two), was that they couldn't believe I had taken the easy option of a C-section...

Forgive me, but I am not sure how I could push an almost 9lb baby out - bum first!

Let me make this perfectly clear. There is no easy option when it comes to giving birth, whether your baby weighs 2lb or over 10lb, if your labour lasts 30 minutes or three days and whether you have a natural delivery or assisted delivery, you are amazing and what you have just achieved is incredible.

DO NOT LET ANYBODY TELL YOU ANY DIFFERENT.

I'd like to say that my story is uncommon, but the likelihood is you will come across people who will make comments without thinking of the consequence and people will always give advice, mostly good, but some not.

Thanks to these stupid remarks, the nervousness of being a new Mum, learning to breastfeed my little one (this is my greatest accomplishment after persevering for six weeks of feeling uncomfortable and cluster feeding- Sebastian went through growth spurts every few weeks and wanted breast milk every hour for 4 or 5 solid hours), sleep deprivation, and recovering from my operation - everything came to a crescendo. I had a big cry, took a deep breath, finally asked for help and advice and eventually feeds became easier, enjoyable and rewarding. Sleep improved, my body healed and I realised I was doing an exceptional job and no-one was going to tell me any different.

Times will be tough, but if you keep positive people around you and accept help, the good will outweigh the bad. Believe me xxx

Love Zoe

KNOW it will pass

Dear New Mother

Being petrified of giving birth led me to enrolling on an amazing hypnobirthing course which transformed my fears and within a few hours of doing the course we were even considering a home birth! I did have him in hospital but I felt so empowered, strong and prepared for whatever was about to come. I channelled my inner hippy and hypno-birthed to the max. It was a huge challenge but knowing that I was designed to give birth and I was the best person to keep my baby calm and safe, gave me a determination and self belief that I didn't know I had. It was unbelievable and I often think about the positive affirmations I learnt. Importantly, my husband James had a clear role, and in that room during the birth, we became this tight knit team that can conquer whatever is thrown at us.

I started to use these positive affirmations a few months after Tommy was born but often still have to remind myself that I am his mum and I know him better than anyone. I am his teacher, his carer and I love him more than anyone else can possibly imagine. I have to trust that I know what is best for him and he needs me no matter what.

I wish I'd started trusting my instincts sooner but everyone tells you so many different ways that things should be done. Remember, it's up to you to listen to what works best for you. It's trial and error. Obsessing over getting Tommy in to a routine at three days old wasn't my finest moment and added lots of stress. I knew I was being silly but books and online posts were harping on about routines and I was really tired. I wanted to sit, feed, cuddle and watch boxsets in those first weeks, but for some reason, I didn't allow myself that normal pleasure. It would have been so special but I felt I needed to be seen as coping and pushed myself to go to baby classes/cafes/meet ups straightaway. I wish I'd spent a few weeks getting strong again as giving birth is a huge thing that is really underplayed nowadays. I felt I should know what I'm doing and people kindly telling me how great a mum I would be, just made me panic and feel judged even more. I couldn't see how I could be 100% responsible for loving, teaching and looking after someone else, particularly when that person would be a tiny, helpless little person for quite a while.

I also wondered how on earth I'd find time to put my make up on before leaving the house – an unanswered question that really did bother me, as I wanted to still feel like me! I found a way and Tommy still likes to play with my make up each morning whilst I get ready!

Having a colicky baby with reflux, who couldn't lie down and cried for around six hours every night for the first 10 weeks was a challenge. James' tip during these awful crying periods would be to buy noise-cancelling headphones! He walked around the room with a screaming Tommy on his shoulder, listening to whatever and I sat gently rocking on the sofa until it stopped! It did stop eventually, just like everyone said it would but that was a tough one.

I had to have an operation for a prolapsed bladder when Tommy was 10 weeks old. I was breastfeeding and the thought of leaving him for four days and not being able to pick him up afterwards was so scary. I worried that he'd forget me; that no one else could look after him, wind him properly or sing the right songs to settle him. It was a hard time and took time for me to adjust to the fact that he was in fact fine. He was being looked after by his dad so I need not worry. I learnt that I could hand over responsibility (reluctantly) and he was still safe and thriving.

It's ok to hugely dislike your husband at times, for whatever silly reason, because there are a hundred other times that the love and respect overflow, and we both have the same goals and aspirations for Tommy and as parents.

It's all a phase. Perhaps my catchphrase forever! It certainly will be for the next baby that is due in seven weeks. I'll be reading this back to myself in those first few dark weeks and taking my own advice. The great thing about the second time – I'm not as scared (more apprehensive!) and I know it will all be ok as time passes, and the next stage begins – for better or for worse! xxx

Love

Kathryn ♡

KNOW you did it!

Dear Mum

Just a note to say...you did it! All those days, weeks, months of waiting have come to this. And as they told you all along, nothing could prepare you for the rush of love you are experiencing. It really is like nothing else. The best and most important piece of advice I could give you, darling mother, is this. Look closely into your baby's eyes. Really close. What do you see? Yes! It's you. All the best bits of you, the pure bits, the real you, before life happened. All wrapped up in your little bundle of joy. So it follows... please never forget to love yourself. Be kind, you have achieved a miracle! Forgive the changes that have allowed your body to accomplish this. Accept the adjustments that will now become inevitable, to you, your life, your decisions. Let the changes ebb and flow like a beautiful river. You may feel sometimes that you as you were lost. Trust me, you are found. Everything that you are and have achieved will enable you to take a breath and acknowledge this huge achievement. Cherish yourself, as, when you are well and happy, so is your precious one. Finally trust....in you, your baby and in the bigger picture. Everything will be ok. It is this trust that will see you through the happy times, and also the sad, tired and lonely times. You are AMAZING.

Love, love, love from one to another

Emma x

Learn to

- accept
- accept help
- be guilt-free
- enjoy yourself

"Love as powerful as your mother's for you leaves its own mark. ... To have been loved so deeply ... will give us some protection forever."

—J. K. Rowling

LEARN to accept

My dearest friends, sisters and fellow-mamas, I begin with a little reminder for you. You are strong, amazing and most of all unique. Remember this as you travel, because it is this uniqueness that gives the world colour; it is this uniqueness that will give your children strength.

I guess if you are reading this letter you are about to embark on the most powerful, fulfilling journey ever, that of motherhood. As you start out, you may be reflecting on your own experiences of family-life, of childhood, and expectations. You might be feeling scared of how your past has shaped your future, and how this will play out in your role as a mama. You may be worried because you are unsure of how to be a mama, and cannot remember great experiences… after all, we are led to believe that we are products of our childhoods. This feels such a powerful and overwhelming responsibility, and one that may make you feel as though you are not on an equal-footing, and one where you believe your child will never be. This is not the case.

Statistically, my realities of motherhood, and that of my children should have resulted in such poor outcomes. After all, I was a teenage mother, I had poor family support, a limited social network and I was a trauma survivor. However, I became a mother, and this was the greatest, most amazing experience. I did not listen to other's expectations of me, I just knew what I could be. Being a mum is not easy for anyone, and I believe your past does not have to shape your future. Even if we have never truly been loved or treasured, this does not mean you are not able to do so. As mamas we can overcome obstacles that may seem impossible. We will face challenges that are new, scary and leave us feeling lonely. But remember you are not alone. You have your child who believes in you and sees you through the eyes of the innocent. Your child's viewpoint will not have been tainted. Your child believes in you like no other. Your child loves your uniqueness, your smell, your smile, your touch, your being. Your child loves you as the person you have become, and by returning that love and acceptance, you will form a bond that can never be broken.

I began this letter, with the words, 'my dearest friends, sisters and fellow-mamas', for a reason. Your child is not the only one who believes in you as a mama. I do. I do so, completely. Without judgment, with openness, trust and belief. Learn to trust your instincts, knowing you have been given a magical gift. The gift of connection. The path will not be easy, but it can be travelled. As a mama, you will never reach your destination, but when possible take the time to enjoy the view. Do not let other's insecurities add to your own – we all have plenty. Being a mama is the most natural thing ever. Being a perfect mama is not. It will not all come easily, but then the best things never do. Acknowledge and accept the negativity, joy and challenges that come with being a mama – and by doing so, you can learn to accept yourself in your new role. Learn to accept your child for who they are, and they, in turn, will learn to accept you. Enjoy.

Love Jen

LEARN to accept help

Dear Lovely New Mums,

When I was expecting my first baby I had all the pregnancy and birth books, I made lists, I joined pregnancy forums, I went to pregnancy yoga, I went to aqua-natal, attended the ante-natal classes and I wrote my birth plan- even down to what music would be played. I thought I was prepared for labour, birth and motherhood…. oh how I laugh at that thought now!

When my little boy decided to arrive four weeks early he took us by surprise, but the biggest surprise for me was that sudden overwhelming feeling. I had read about the overwhelming feeling of love you have when you give birth, but for me everything was overwhelming.

I loved my teeny tiny newborn son completely but nothing could prepare me for the sudden responsibility that the new little life brings with them when they come into the world. I felt sheer panic. I didn't know how to change a nappy, didn't have a clue if I was feeding correctly and wasn't sure how to stop the tiny squawks that seemed relentless. That feeling of being overwhelmed continued for a little while especially as I tried to establish feeding as my poor little boy would be shrieking in pain. I didn't know it at the time but he had colic, reflux and what turned out to be a milk allergy. All these problems served for relentless sleepless nights and that didn't help to make me feel any less emotional and overwhelmed. I sought help from the health visitor and my lovely GP about all of my baby's issues and after making another emotional decision to stop breastfeeding and bottle feed on prescription milk (there were many tears over this) life got better for our little family.

Of course, looking back I was hormonal so every small issue felt like a mountain and all newborn babies cry as they adjust to their new world whether they are perfectly fine, suffering with colic or digestion problems. Those first few weeks are as overwhelming for them as it is for the new parents. We are all adjusting to this new life.

My advice to those embarking on motherhood is to accept help whenever you need it. Whether this is from your partner, parents, in-laws, family and friends or health visitor/GP. Please don't feel that you have to be superwoman and be the perfect "yummy mummy" with the perfectly clean house and a contented baby. The perfect mum is a myth and we as women put ourselves under so much unnecessary pressure. All that matters is that you and your baby are happy and healthy.

Lots of love and luck in your new chapter

Becky

LEARN to be guilt free

Dear New Mother,

I have carried you and kept you safe
Felt every kick and elbow in the wrong place
I can't wait to meet you but what do I do?
Where is the manual, the instructions, the how to?

The nursery is ready with clothes clean and pressed
The hospital bag by the door must not get left
How could someone so small need so much stuff?
They don't you will soon realise, all they need is your love

Now you are here and the waiting is over
The real journey starts, try and keep your composure
Your touch is their world, your voice the best thing
Oxytocin is flowing and the bond will begin

For some love comes easily, the bond strong at the start
For others it takes time, but will come from the heart
Cuddle, touch, stroke, massage and sing
Carry, rock, sway, snuggle and swing

The nights can seem endless and the crying so loud
It is ok to ask for help, please don't be too proud
Speak to family, friends, try and take a break
Get some fresh air, have a walk, for your own sanity's sake

Realign your expectations of what you can achieve in a day
A clean, well fed, warm baby scores high anyway
Still in your pyjamas at the lunchtime news?
Who cares? Does not matter, you're then ready to snooze

You won't spoil a baby with love and affection
They don't know how to manipulate or cause deception
Their cry is their way to let you know something is wrong
Dirty nappy, hungry, tired, cuddles or sing me a song

Am I doing this right? Why can't my baby do that?
There is no one size fits all, remember that fact
Try not to judge others who aren't doing the same
Trusting *your* instincts is the name of the game

Penny Sibthorp

LEARN to enjoy it

Dear Mama,

Welcome to the world of motherhood - a crazy, exciting, wonderful world that I never knew existed before my little one was born. Motherhood is a huge adventure, a new exciting challenge – tiring, beautiful, hard work and full of love all in the same breath.

For me, motherhood has been a journey that I was really not prepared for and a lot harder than I expected. To be honest, I really don't know what I expected when I decided that I wanted to become a mother, but what has been surprising is just how much it has changed me as a woman and altered the course of my life. I hope this does the same to you too. Whether you are a pregnant mama or a new mama with a tiny newborn looking to gain advice, I would like to say that motherhood is an awesome journey and I am so glad that you have decided to enter the most special phase of your life so far.

Now some of you may think – special phase? Awesome journey? Love? – seriously – I'm shattered, tired, broken, exhausted, confused, unprepared, crying all the time, anxious… Don't worry, that's perfectly normal and perfectly ok. I was there. I felt those feelings, had those thoughts and cried those tears too.

Becoming a mother is not easy.
Becoming a mother does not come easy.
Becoming a mother may never be easy.

But becoming a mother is like discovering a superpower that has been lying dormant for years. If you trust your intuition, you will know what to do and you will be the amazing mother that I know you can be.

Here in the UK, society and the media seem to think that women can be perfect mothers, have the perfect career, have the perfect body, and rear the perfect child – oh, and do it all with minimal support. Really? And just what is perfect? Why do we have all this pressure? It's so unfair and so impossible. It takes more than one person to raise a child – it takes a family, a community - it takes help and support. So when you need help mama, ASK FOR IT! Call in all those favours. Don't ever feel like you have to struggle on your own. Asking for help is not failing – it is being wise. It is doing the best for your baby.

As for balancing work and your baby – just do your best. Take your time. Breathe, stop and enjoy. These first few months only happen once and although tiring and exhausting and demanding both physically and mentally, your baby is only a baby once. Never worry what other people think or say – just do what you can and if you can't do it, does it really matter?

Now, don't even start me on the post-baby body stuff. As a yoga teacher myself I am very aware of the pressure on new mums, including myself to "get back into shape" after the baby has arrived. What does this even mean? I have a shape. It might be a different shape to before baby arrived, but I have a shape. Is it any worse than before? Hell no! NEWS FLASH - I just grew a whole human being. The milk I produce feeds my baby and is her 100% source of sustenance (and that did not come easy - don't start me on support and help for breastfeeding and new mums either). Do I fit into pre-baby clothes? Nope, with a capital N, but I have the superpower to create life and sustain it. Beat that Superman! I wouldn't change an inch of me and nor should you. Maybe I should eat a little less cake but hell

I'm tired, so I think I'm allowed a few treats and so are you mama.

I also want to say that everything will be ok. Take one day at a time. Every tiny success is a win for team mama. If you manage a shower today – go you. If you manage to get your baby to sleep – go you. If you manage a lucid conversation with another adult today – go you. If you finally manage to breastfeed without problems (breastfeeding is NOT EASY!) – go you. If you finally get your baby to take a bottle – go you! If you sleep when baby sleeps or do any little modicum of housework – go you! Any success, however small – go you! Whatever decisions you make, whatever route you choose, whatever you feel and struggle with, it's all ok. Give yourself a break, give yourself some rest and look after yourself you precious creature you.

You are amazing,
You are a life-creator.
You are doing your best and that is perfection.
You are a mama.

With love, hugs and bags of chocolate buttons.

Susan Yeates, Yoga teacher and new mama

Remember

- nobody knows what they are doing
- to love yourself
- to practise self-love
- to learn together
- to dream big
- to count your blessings

"There's no way to be a perfect mother and a million ways to be a good one."
—Jill Churchill

REMEMBER nobody knows what they are doing

Dear Mama,

I have been a mother for nearly seven years now and I will let you into a secret (not so secret)… I have no idea what I'm doing. Truth be told, I'm not confident in giving advice on most aspects of life but I am a mother so here goes.

"Expectant Mother" is used to describe pregnant women. Expectant I certainly was. Expectant that I would have a baby. Expectant that said baby would become a child and that child would be certain way. Expectant that I would live a certain lifestyle. I thought it was my job to achieve this, so, wonderful beautiful women, I invite you now to let go of your expectations. I know they are inevitable but what are the chances of them becoming reality? Not one of mine has materialised (thank goodness). This is a good thing, a great thing. I would not change my experience to make it that of my pre-baby dreams. What I have now is far too awesome.

I now have two exceptional children born within 13 months of each other. The joy and love they have brought into my life is indescribable. I'm learning and growing everyday, from being their mother. Each new day brings an adventure and I attempt to meet it with enthusiasm. I can't deny that a lot of this adventure has brought with it a new kind of fear that I had no previous experience of.

Mostly, it's joyful and intoxicating and filled with songs, smiles, tears, cuddles, dancing and the best conversations ever. My children give me a new perspective on life as they see it from such different angles to me and each other. There is such beauty in exploring this world from a fresh point of view. This has helped me to shred some unconscious judgments I held. Having a point of view is important but exploring and examining these views is essential.

My first lesson - don't panic that nothing is under control! One of the harshest experiences as a new mother was when my youngest daughter became ill just two weeks after her entrance to the world. I'd had my beautiful home birth where I did it all my way. I felt empowered and connected to my new born girl and then within a flash, everything was taken from my hands. Literally, she was in hospital for what seemed (at the time) a lifetime and I couldn't hold her. I couldn't feed her. I had no control over what might happen. I had never known helplessness until that point. This was when I really learnt first hand, the power of touch or, unfortunately in our case, the lack of it. My baby girl did get better, we left the hospital and I held her close in my arms for the next five years. What I took from this, was the realisation that I can't control this life stuff for them, like I expected I would.

After our return home I was told that there was a strong possibility that she would have additional needs. This is when I came face to face with the next expectation. The expectation of what my child would be, again I'd believed wholeheartedly that I would also be in charge of that. I was not! As a mother I've found it infinitely difficult to let go! What helps me, is to remember that my children are not my children. I do not own my daughters. They are not mine; they never were because they are their very own soul, belonging to no one and everyone at the same time. My children are the responsibility of the world. It's not all on me. Shockingly, some of it is on them.

We can not and should not control the lives of our children. We can not protect them from life. We can not and should not attempt to change them in any way.

What we do own is our motherhood - that is ours and it is something invaluable and powerful. We do control our love and our responses to life's ups and downs. What do children need? Love? Connection? Space to become everything they already are? There it is…we can not 'make' our children loving, happy, peaceful, kind or intelligent humans. We can however give them the gift of living an authentic life. We give our children joy when we are joyful. When we love ourselves and take time out to be true to ourselves, we teach our children to do the same. We are our children's teachers so be love, show love and accept love.

If you hear yourself say I can't do this, just remember you already are!

Remember, I love you, that you are everything and you've got this! Good luck and thank you for indulging me.

Love L ♡

REMEMBER to love yourself

Dear New Mummy,

I remember it like it was yesterday. I was a young, naive 17 years old desperate for love and for somebody to love me back, starved of affection with low self-esteem.

I fell in love with her instantly but quickly the realisation dawned on me. This was no fairytale and all was not fixed with her arrival- she didn't bring the magic key. What she did bring was sleepless nights. She brought excessive crying. She brought judgement from others and especially from myself.

Life was hard and I was alone. My confidence plummeted to an all-time low and without a support network, my days were a bottomless pit of misery and shame. At my lowest point, I considered giving her up or taking my own life. The memories of that time are too painful to bear, I was alone and scared, a baby playing at being a mother.

I wish I could say how I got out of that place so that it could help others, but in all honesty, I think it was just time. She grew older and easier to manage and by the time I was expecting my second daughter I was petrified of history repeating itself but also determined that this time it would be different.

This time I was the mother who succeeded at breastfeeding and got through those painful first weeks, I was the mother who held my daughter constantly - not to try to silence her cries but because I enjoyed her company. I was the one taking her out and showing her off with a smile not looking at others and comparing myself, scared that I was being judged. I was the mother who took her to baby massage classes to further strengthen our bond and massaged her every night after her bath as I said the words, "thank God for my baby," and kissed her soft head. I felt truly grateful that I had been given a second chance and enjoyed every minute of her instead of the guilt of wishing her life away.

Fast forward 18 years after having my first and I'm pregnant again. A much-desired baby, the result of IVF. If you had told that sad young girl back then that not only would she have a third but she would go to such measures to have it, she would have thought you were crazy, but here I am with my third daughter on the way and I couldn't be happier.

I look at how my other two have grown, one already a woman and the other not far behind and I couldn't be more proud, not only of them but of the job I have done raising them and of raising myself at the same time and I feel sure that this time I will be fine, this time I am not afraid.

If I could go back and see myself in those dark, lonely days, I would give myself a hug, I would scoop myself up, wipe away the tears and reassure myself that it will all work out ok and to just hang in there, I would say I am worthy of love but that first I need to learn to love myself.

Love Jade ♡

REMEMBER to practise self - love

5 THINGS TO DO BEFORE YOU LOSE YOUR S***!

Motherhood is beautiful and rewarding but it can be terrifying and draining. Becoming a parent often reveals our best qualities but it can also on occasion rear our ugly side. In the three years since becoming a mother (you may be thinking, hmmm… that's not very long) it is surprising the amount of knowledge I have amassed, especially regarding how to avoid losing my shit and attempting to keep everything together. The following five tips are how I am not only surviving, but loving motherhood.

Number 1 - Breathe

Count to ten close your eyes and repeat: this moment will pass. Your baby will stop crying, your toddler will stop having a tantrum, your teenager does still need you and you will eventually sleep. I'm still not convinced of the last one but I'm sure I will one day! Always remember the beautiful, priceless moments will outweigh the low points and nothing lasts forever.

Number 2 - Cuddle

When was the last time you had a good snuggle? Take a minute and have a cuddle. Whoever it is - your babies, your partner, your family or friends. Even if they are the source of your anger, frustration or sadness. It is important to slow down and feel the love. Having a good squeeze will instantly calm you down and help release any stress.

Number 3 – Hydrate and Eat

When did you last have a glass of water and something to eat? If it's been a few hours, go to the kitchen and eat and drink something! No one likes a hangry dehydrated Mama. You cannot function properly. Preferably something healthy, which will make you feel much better but I'd be lying if I didn't say my diet consists mainly of tea and biscuits. On a side note if it is Friday and after 6pm whiskey or wine is acceptable and if you made it to Friday before having a drink you are winning!

Number 4 – Connect

Where is your village? Every so often we all need to rant and share and realise we aren't going loco. Realise you are not alone, accept your feelings and most importantly tell your truth. Stop answering, "I'M OKAY". Elaborate, connect and share the good times and the bad. Stop being a martyr (guilty), accept and ask for help - if and when you need it. Life is so much easier when you surround yourself with amazing people.

Number 5 – Move

I'm not necessarily talking full on exercise, unless you choose to - if so, Go You! Every day try to move as much as you can, walk, get some fresh air, if it's a duvet kind of day then dance, and I mean dance like no one is watching - without a care in the world. The children will love it, everyone loves a dance party, the crazier the moves, all the better. Choose music that transports you to your happy place. If it is possible plug your headphones in and listen to your favourite songs, I do this during my rare soaks in the bath and it is heaven! Try and find some headspace, practice Yoga. If that's a bit too much then just try some gentle stretches, do whatever it is that helps you unwind and switch off. Make time for what makes you feel happy even if it's just for a moment out of your busy life.

Final note – Judgment and Competition.

Humans judge naturally, the same goes for competition - it's in our nature and it can motivate us to become our best self but please, please, please try not to compare yourself and most importantly your children, to others. We are all unique individuals and that is our greatest power. We all pass judgment, we do it even when we try not to, and yes, everyone is entitled to their own opinion but, and it's a BIG BUT, please try your hardest to only think it and do not share your negative thoughts or gossip about another mother or parent - remember you don't know them and even if you do know them it's not helpful to share any negative thoughts about who they are and how they parent. We are all on a journey where we have had to make choices, some of which have come easily, but many of which are hard choices - you don't know their circumstances and the reasons behind these choices. The best thing you can do is start a conversation and try to be supportive.

Motherhood is different for everyone we are all on our own adventure, have faith that most parents are just doing the best they can do for their family and as a mum that's all you can do.

Jessica Rothenberg

REMEMBER to learn together

Dear New Mummy,

Looking back over my nearly 20 years as a mummy, my only dream was to be a perfect mummy. As a naïve and shy 19-year-old, first time mummy, I was unprepared for the overwhelming feelings of love and responsibility as my first little boy was placed in my arms, the love was nothing like I'd experienced before and I knew I'd found my happy place in becoming a mummy. Connor was an easy going baby and life settled as I married his dad a few years later and began to think about baby number two.

Getting pregnant again wasn't so easy and we experienced heartbreak along the way, my pregnancy with my second son wasn't so smooth. The stress took its toll and I ended up with Bell's palsy, a facial paralysis that affected my left side of my face. A few days later I was to get the surprise of my life as I went to the bathroom without any sign of labour only to emerge a few minutes later with my second baby boy. Giving birth alone so quickly sent me into shock, I had no labour, I was totally unprepared. I had everyone telling me how lucky I was, so I quickly blanked out the awful dark thoughts and feelings I had. I should be grateful I had another beautiful boy, I hadn't gone through the pain of labour, but my goodness how I felt was so painful.

The next few months were a blur Reagan had colic and reflux and would scream and cry constantly day and night. I was his mummy I should be able to help him and comfort him, looking at the pain in his face I was convinced he hated me and I probably scared him looking as I did. I knew deep down that I fiercely loved this little boy but I didn't feel I was enough for him, I'd failed him, oh my goodness you should see him now mummy. He is the most level-headed, kind-hearted, responsible, generous and loving fifteen-year-old I know. If only I had someone telling me that it was going to be ok on those long lonely nights holding him tight and pacing the bedroom floor.

We then had my third son 20 months later with another speedy arrival at home, he was a little angel bless him and all he did was sleep. Over the next few years, I would find myself trapped alone with dark thoughts and feelings, sleep deprived and thoroughly exhausted I was lost. However I told no one, I kept up the pretence I was ok, I was alright, I had to be the perfect mum and wife. I painted on the lipstick and carried on, although I pushed my husband away resulting in us splitting up for a while.

We did get back together after some time but I had to face up to the hard fact of admitting that I had postnatal depression and had done for five years. Admitting it was hard but talking and asking for help saved me, discovering I was pregnant again with my fourth son left me a little nervous. I was prepared for another speedy arrival, he didn't let us down rushing into the world in the bedroom two weeks early. This time around I was filled with feelings of calmness and love and I finally accepted that I am an imperfect mummy. So as I sit here with my fifth baby boy watching him sleep with an overwhelming sense of love you would think I've got it sussed. No mummy, life with five boys is crazy, unpredictable and at times tough, sometimes I don't get it right but that's ok, they are ok too, watching them grow and find their way in life just fills my heart with love and pride.

New mummy my advice to you, let go of perfect, let go of striving to be super-mum - they don't exist. Just sit, relax and breathe in the wonderfulness you have created. Believe in yourself, you are enough for your baby and it truly is ok to be 'not ok'. Talk, talk and talk some more and don't be afraid to ask for help. So whether this is your first or your fifth baby each baby is unique and what works for one baby may not work for another, each one will leave their footprints forever etched in your heart. Babies don't come with a manual and there isn't one for a mummy too, together you will find your way trust in your instincts but most of all enjoy the wonder and possibilities of your new beginning.

Lots of love

Claire xx

REMEMBER to dream big (1)

Dear New Mum,

I have sat down to write this letter so many times over the last few weeks and I'm finding it hard. This is a surprise to me as I write this letter in my head all the time. Yet now it is the time to put pen to paper or fingers to MacBook, it feels very different.

I think it is because seeing the words in front of me touches my heart so deeply. To look upon the journey that motherhood has afforded me. The highs and the lows, the joy and the tears.

My journey to motherhood was a difficult one, multiple miscarriages and an abnormal reproductive system meant I thought it would never happen. I know there are some of you reading this who have also been in similar positions experiencing similar feelings.

I am so very grateful to now be the mother of a beautiful, energetic and (as stubborn as her father) four year old girl. It was the difficulty of conceiving that made it hard to 'not be okay' in the beginning and to admit that this was both the hardest and the best wish to ever come true.

What I know for sure is that your intuition is guiding you, just as mine was guiding me and she'll never do you wrong. I believe motherhood heightens our inner voice but then so many things can work against it...Google, the in-laws, the well-meaning advice ...I could go on and on.

Don't think because you didn't know something, or because it didn't quite go the way you planned it, that you are somehow a failure. You aren't. You are all kinds of wonderful, you are doing your best and you are more than enough.

Dreaming was one of the many surprises of motherhood. I have always been a day-dreamer. Ever since a little girl I could be found in my own dream world, seeing in my mind everything from a trip to Disney to making a difference to women around the world and of course meeting Oprah along the way.

Yet before I became a Mum, it was all reserved strictly for dreamland and it was when that child exited my body and entered the world and I realised what I had done, that dreams started to look a lot more possible. Whether you had the same or not, don't worry. Just know that you have done an amazing thing! You are capable of more and different amazing things IF that's what you choose to do.

For me, birthing my baby gave me the permission I thought I needed to create a life that I loved in all areas. Now that I had the child I longed for, I was ready. Amongst the sleep exhaustion, the sore nipples, the tears and the hard times, there are the cuddles, laughs and love but also within that are your dreams. Your desires for how you want to be. And note I say 'be' because as much as I am a doer as I'm sure you are too. At this time it is about being with your dreams and seeing what happens. For some of you, it might be springing into action and creating something…anything. For others, it will be about being. Neither is better or worse than the other. They are both valid.

As this letter draws to a close, I just want to let you know that you're amazing and I invite you to say it to yourself, right now, as you read these words… 'I am amazing'. And then repeat it and do what you need to do to be able to see it every day.

Write it on a post-it and stick it to the bathroom mirror, add it is as an alert on your phone, put a note in your baby's changing bag. I know you probably don't say it to yourself very often, if ever. But it's the truth. You are amazing!

With love,

Nicola X x

REMEMBER to dream big (2)

Dear Mummy

One of my greatest adventures was visiting the Amazon Rainforest and standing under the Great Kapok tree! It is a giant tree whose highest branch seems to project into outer space and tickle the stars. Its roots are like mountains as they rise from the ground creating areas to shelter and nestle into. Ivy creeps and climbs around and up its trunk but the Kapok tree is too mighty, too strong to let these climbers bother it. Tarzan-like vines dangle down from dizzy heights inviting you to have a little play, a little swing. It is magical!

I am telling you this because you are your family's Kapok tree. You are giving life to your beautiful baby. You are offering a safe place to nestle into and you will be their first play mate.

Like Motherhood the Kapok tree is sacred. It is trusted by many animals, insects and plants who call it their home and their source of life. Trust, it's a big deal in many different areas of life and it will become a big deal within your exploration of motherhood. In fact, you have already been nurturing and growing trust as you grow your baby.

Trusting your body to nurture and grow your baby and allowing your 'Maternal instinct' to guide you is really important and can be extremely empowering. Be strong like the Kapok tree and don't allow the 'you should be' to irritate or affect you.

Focus on freeing your mind up from those vines so that you can be true to your unique Mama flow. Have the confidence to back yourself (from experience I know sleep deprivation and hormones can get in the way of this at times), your ideas and your beliefs. If you feel a little lacking in confidence then why not try;

Talking to a like-minded friend/peer/online group....(it's important that you do this in a setting that allows you to gain confidence not to feel more inhibited).
Research facts, science etc. and reflect on how this matches to your instincts.
Find a parent blogger you resonate with.
Explore different mother/father and baby classes.
Reflect and write things out and down. Communicate with your partner/family about your ideas. Something that really helped me was to back my ideas with science. This really helped me feel empowered to explain my reasons for any of my parenting choices with confidence.

Allow your Mama flow to shine through and guide you. You are the Kapok tree, you grew your baby, you are continuing to give life to your baby and you are your baby's first friend.

No one knows your baby and you better than yourself.

Believe, Trust & Love.

Xx Colette

REMEMBER to count your blessings

To all the new mothers who have been blessed with a child with Down Syndrome,

I am writing this letter to share my story, to give you much needed hope and strength. My story starts in 2012, sitting in a car park with my husband, having just received the news that my baby had Down Syndrome. I never would have expected this would happen to me at the age of 31. My husband and I were both shocked. We both cried for the loss of a child that we thought we were going to have. We didn't realise that our lives would never be the same again.

The next few months were tough. Not only were there many complications and ongoing scans, we were also faced with the negativity of doctors. One 'specialist' told us that our child would be severely retarded and we were offered to terminate more than once. He made us feel that it would be unnatural to continue with my pregnancy, knowing what we did. However, we had both decided we were going to go ahead. This has happened for a reason. I thought, and I was determined to be the best mother that I could be. It was my duty to protect my baby.

I started researching more about Down Syndrome, ordering books and signing up to associations. I had no idea what to expect but I know I had a supportive husband and family and I had a loving bond already growing, between me and my baby. I used to speak to my baby everyday and tell him that I loved him and everything was going to be ok. "Mama loves you," I used to say, rubbing my belly.

My beautiful son was born at 32 weeks by a planned c-section. As soon as I saw him, it was love at first sight. It felt surreal. There he was, my little baby boy and he was absolutely perfect! He weighed only three pounds and was soon transferred to an incubator and taken to the neonatal ward, where he stayed for five weeks. It was a few days later when I actually got to hold him. The nurse explained to me about Kangaroo Care, which was skin to skin contact to help control his temperature and develop our mother baby bond. She helped me place him carefully in my vest and what a wonderful experience it was! I instantly felt a rush of oxytocin and as I looked down at his beautiful little face, I whispered, "I love you." He responded by moving his head up and it felt like he made a sigh, as if to say, "finally, my mummy is here". It was a very emotional experience.

Time has flown by so quickly and I cannot believe that he is going to be five years old. There has always been a tremendous amount of support available to us and there are ongoing appointments from paediatricians, audiologists, ophthalmologists, physiotherapists, speech and language therapists, cardiologists...the list goes on.

In June last year, he had open heart surgery. The worst nightmare for any parent but we couldn't believe how quickly he recovered. He is such a strong and brave little boy. He has accomplished many things that normal children do but it has taken him a little longer to get there. He has started school and made friends. He starred as Joseph in his first Christmas nativity play and a few months ago he started taking his first steps. On a recent holiday to Cyprus, we were so proud to see him on stage, dancing around with all of the other children. He has bought so much happiness into our lives. He has a wonderful sense of humour, is lovable, affectionate, sociable and he loves making others laugh. His smile is truly infectious. He has made me a stronger person, taught me to appreciate the little things and love life. He is perfect and I wouldn't change him for the world. It has not always been easy of course but when is it ever easy to raise a child?

So, to all of you mothers out there, don't be disheartened or scared or worried. Be happy and be strong and celebrate your new bundle of joy. Everything will be fine. Try and enjoy every single moment and capture photos and videos to treasure. There is a supportive community of parents out there to help and guide you every step of the way. Every child is different, embrace their uniqueness. Every child is a gift from up above. That's the meaning behind my son's name, Niam.

Love from a proud mother xxx

Aarti Bagha

Enjoy

- your achievements
- each and every chapter

"There is such a special sweetness in being able to participate in creation."

Pamela S. Nadav

ENJOY your achievements

Dear New Mother,

As I sit here on the eve of my eldest daughter's ninth birthday I've been reminiscing and sharing memories.

I don't recall ever having specific expectations, all I've ever wanted since I was a little girl was to be a Mum. So once I'd moved out it seemed natural for that to be the next move.

My beautiful little girl was born at 38 weeks. All went perfectly fine until, after two hours of pushing, it became evident she wasn't budging. Cue a rush to the theatre, spinal block administered and a forceps delivery attempted. After 15 hours of labour all I remember is a tugging sensation then a crash and people running past me as the Doctor slipped over, literally pulling my baby from my body and causing a fourth-degree tear to myself.

It all seems a blur now but at the time it meant that her first year was a blur of hospital appointments, reconstructive surgery and counselling.

If anything though it made our bond amazingly strong. She was mine, my baby and I wasn't going to let anyone hurt her again.

After the trauma of her delivery, it took four years to even think about having another baby. And when I did fall pregnant I sadly lost my baby at six weeks. It was hard and I still think about this little one all the time.

My second daughter was delivered by contrast in an amazingly calm and lovely elective C-section and despite growing up and discovering she has numerous special needs and learning difficulties she continues to live her life as an extremely chilled out, affectionate little girl.

I always laughed when people said to make the most of every minute when they are small because it will fly by. The sleepless nights, the long, lonely days of maternity leave, the colic, the crying, all made each day seem never ending. Yet here I am wondering where on earth the last nine years have gone? That tiny little baby, left battered and bruised, is now making her way in the world and making me proud every step of the way. My youngest daughter may not have the same opportunities or achieve what we had dreamt for her but we love her so much and have learnt to see the world through completely different eyes.

Their dad left when she was three months old and I can't lie. At times it was ridiculously hard. He's no longer part of their lives through his own choosing. But I made it through and have since met the most amazing man who has shown me what happiness is and taught me how to make the most of every opportunity. Together with his two children, our family is complete.

And that's how we live life. We are laidback, calm, appreciate the little things and celebrate every achievement. We embrace all that life throws at us. The bonds created in our family are strong, unbreakable and formed by love, trust, respect and a little bit of craziness.

Appreciate every second you are blessed with, see the positive in every situation, celebrate the smallest of achievements, try not to have expectations - live in the now. Don't compare yourself to others, be yourself and learn who you are as your journey as a Mum progresses and you get to know your baby. Live life and be happy ♡

Love Sarah

ENJOY each and every chapter

Dear New Mum,

I am writing this in the middle of a pretty good day. I had a half decent sleep last night; just one-night feed at 3 am and then a morning 6:30 am feed. My three-month-old even had an hour's nap late morning which meant I could hoover, wash the dishes, and prep tonight's food before the rest of the clan come home (rock and roll, right?). She is now happily kicking away on her play mat... Oh, hang on, there's a poop situation going on, be right back (not even joking)!

So as I was saying, she is happily kicking on her play mat which is how I have time to sit and write this; with a hot cup of tea, I might add! Sounds like I've got my shiz together, doesn't it? Rewind to yesterday morning...

I woke up feeling absolutely exhausted! Baby went down to sleep earlier than usual (not that she has a routine - but I thought I was winning with this one), but she also woke up for her next feed earlier than usual - approximately one hour after I put my head down, ouch! Then there were idiots racing motorbikes in the distant streets for what felt like hours, then came the sirens, and finally silence! Cue the two middle kids waking up (the other half is on "deal with the older kids during the night when I'm on night feeds" duties, but there was a hell of a commotion going on across the landing). Silence. Closed my eyes. Baby wanted more boob!

So all this resulted in me waking up with a heavy, and seriously foggy head, and I could feel my nerves twitching. Every little sound got on my last nerve; let alone the screaming tantrums of the three-year-old and whining meltdowns of the five-year-old. Throw in the teenager winding them both up and I knew how the day was going to pan out... and it didn't disappoint! Let's just say, I would like to erase the day from my memory. Everything about it was rubbish! We shouted like lunatics at the kids for shouting like lunatics at each other. Then felt guilty about shouting like lunatics and not leading by example, then we shouted some more. We snapped at each other. I huffed and puffed and could very well have blown the house down with my stinking mood. The baby couldn't cope with the two middle ones being so loud so she was on edge, wanting to be held constantly (breaking my back), and either feeding for lengthy periods of time or fussing on the boob. I felt like I could easily have walked out the door and not ever come back, but let's be honest they all would have just followed me anyway!

We made sure the two middle ones were bathed and ready for bed super early, for everyone's sanity (including their own). Their dad put them to bed, the teen took himself to his room to listen to music and do his homework, and I took the smallest one to my bedroom. I stripped her down to her nappy, took a deep breath, and she smiled the biggest, beaming, gummy smile at me. In that second, the house was calm and order was restored.

The point of this letter is to say that you will have utterly crap days.

That is okay.

You will feel guilty about how you handled situations.

That is okay.

You and your partner will say mean things to each other.

That is okay, but you probably should apologise! (Sorry Bedwyr xxx)

You will feel lonely, at your wit's end, beyond exhausted... That is okay because you just don't know what tomorrow might bring.

The good days roll with the bad days. Babies are so unpredictable. I mean we never know ourselves what mood we are going to wake up in! Don't feel like you have to have everything under control, or that you have to be out and about and be "busy". You're busy enough nurturing an actual tiny person! It's only now that I'm on my fourth child I've realised it's ok to say, "You know what, today I do not intend to leave the house." As parents, we put far too much pressure on ourselves, and it's about time we gave ourselves a break.

Enjoy your little one, and enjoy getting to know each other again. Becoming parents changes our priorities and who we are. Enjoy this chapter as a new family, including the crappy moments. One day you will look back and laugh at them.

Welcome to the club!

Lots and lots of love, and lots and lots of luck,

Emma

Do

- talk
- talk, talk and talk some more
- embrace ALL the emotions
- keep your identity
- be yourself
- what you think is best

"Yesterday is gone. Tomorrow is yet to come. We have only today. If we help our children to be what they should be today, they will have the necessary courage to face life with greater love."

- Mother Theresa

DO talk

Dear New Mama,

Congratulations on entering this new and wonderful phase in your life. Everyone will tell you that your life will never be the same, and they're right. You will never love anything else as much as your own child. But, and there is a but, it won't always be sunshine and roses.

I always wanted to be a mum, and am pleased to say that I've had two wonderful pregnancies, which both ended with straightforward, planned home births in a pool in my living room. Bliss. I'm a person who likes to be in control, so for me, they were perfect. But not everything has been such plain sailing.

I was always going to breastfeed. After an easy pregnancy and a relatively easy labour, I wasn't expecting breastfeeding to be hard. Why would it be? But it was. Latching was a nightmare. I ended up expressing colostrum into a teaspoon for my first daughter. I cried. Lots. So did my husband. And our daughter. Luckily, I got great support and we continued breastfeeding past two years. Talking was the key. Talking to my family, and talking to the right people about my breastfeeding struggles. It became so important to me that I trained as a breastfeeding counsellor and now help other mums on their feeding journey.

But that's not all. As much as I loved being a mum, and was happy with my decision to leave my job behind, I found myself struggling with my emotions behind closed doors. When our daughter was about a year old, I realised I needed help. I spoke to my Health Visitor, my GP, my mum and my husband. My mental health was suffering and I was diagnosed with PND, but they helped me through. Again, talking was the key. I had to admit to myself how I felt, and then be willing to talk to others about it.

Shortly before our eldest turned two we decided to start trying for another baby. In a couple of short months I was pregnant and we were over the moon. And then the worst happened. Six days after the Big Fat Positive, I woke up to find I was bleeding heavily. Instantly, I knew that baby was no more. I've never felt more devastated or empty. Just six days, but I'd already created a life for this baby in my heart and mind. It took two days of hospital appointments and tests for it to be officially confirmed, and then I had to accept it all over again. In over ten years together, I've seen my husband cry only a handful of times. I think half of them were that week. My wonderful parents were away on the holiday of a lifetime, so I called my twin brother this time. I had to tell someone. Now I have come to terms with it, I mention the loss whenever it's relevant. Almost everyone has a 'me too' story and it helps to know that it really is common and there's no-one to blame.

Just four weeks after the miscarriage, I was pregnant again. This time there was no fanfare, no celebration, no feelings of joy. Just trepidation and anxiety. Luckily, as the weeks went by, the pregnancy continued and our second daughter was born at home in the water just like her sister. This time she breastfed like a dream. But once again, when she was about eight months old, I realised that I needed some mental health support. I felt overwhelmed. How could something so wonderful – being a mum – be so difficult? Again, I spoke to my husband and my mum, and referred myself for talking therapy support. I still have the occasional bad day, of course, like everyone else, but I don't have to worry any more about my mental health or its impact on my children.

Some women feel that they lose their identity when they become a mum, and I can understand that. For me personally, though, being a mum IS my identity. It's what I'm here for and I couldn't imagine my life any other way. But I'd be lying if I said it's always easy or that I'm never lonely. Talking is key. Talk to your partner about how you feel. Talk to your family members, talk to your children. They need to understand emotions too. And if you need more support, talk to your GP, your Health Visitor, a breastfeeding counsellor, a mental health support worker. Find your tribe and know that whatever you're going through, someone else is going through it too. You're never alone.

And mama, you've got this.

Tam

DO talk, talk and talk some more

Dear Lovely Mummies,

When thinking about this letter, the same feelings seem to flood my body- the excitement, the nerves, the unease and the love. Reflecting back not only gives you clarity but lets you relive it all again.

I am actually going to write about my second baby; I thought that as my first pregnancy and labour were all very straightforward, I assumed the second would be too. There was a relatively short time between the pregnancies so I thought my body would 'fall back' into it all and I had heard that second labours were always so much quicker than the first.

I wasn't expecting my son to be born early and I wasn't expecting a quick labour of just two hours. I was in shock and with adrenaline running through me as they handed me my newest little bundle. I remember just looking at him in almost disbelief that he was here when I least expected him to. I remember looking at his little hands and knowing they just didn't look right. They were blue and very cold. I tried massaging them to help his circulation flow but it didn't seem to work. Then I noticed his hard and laboured breathing that sounded loud and forced in the stillness of the delivery room which had fallen calm after the rush. I alerted the midwives who examined and listened deftly before explaining they would have a consultant have a look 'just to be sure'.

It then felt like only moments later he was being taken away from me; I remember thinking it couldn't be right because I had only just brought him into this world. He was being wheeled down to the Neo-Natal Unit because he needed assistance.

To be honest the rest is almost a blur of nurses, healthcare assistants and paediatricians; he had some fluid in his lungs and needed some help breathing. I remember the first time seeing him in his little incubator with the machines and wires surrounding him. I remember watching him sleeping so quietly and wishing he was sleeping peacefully in my arms.

I spent so much time down at the Neo-Natal Unit because I wanted to be with him very much but also because it was easier to be with him than sitting on the postnatal ward with all the other parents and their new babies, babies who were all going home faster than my baby was. My favourite time to go and see him was during the night. It was quieter and with only two nurses on. They would silently carry on their work whilst I sang to him softly and talked to him and stroked him gently, reassuring him I was still there. It felt like there was no one else in the world except us. Nothing really mattered in those moments except for the two of us and our little world together.

He actually recovered fairly quickly and a week later he was with me back on the postnatal ward and we were discharged shortly after that. Now he is a strong and energetic two and a half-year-old. He amazes me every day, not only with his wonder and excitement of the world but also with his strength to overcome anything that is thrown at him. Sometimes I find myself holding on to him for a few moments longer than hugs usually last, and giving him a little extra squeeze for my own reassurance.

My words of advice are to talk and talk and talk some more. Ask the questions you have about your pregnancy and birth, request a debrief after labour if you think it will help, find out the answers you want to know. I would also say appreciate every day, ordinary moments. Revel in the normality of your daily routine and embrace the small moments together.

I read somewhere once that, 'The days are long but the years are short', and for me, it is so very true.

Embrace the love, enjoy the new beginnings.

Helen xx

DO embrace ALL the emotions

Dear New Mummy,

For a good ten years of my life I did everything to avoid getting pregnant; I mean you only have to have sex once to get pregnant, right? Yet, when the time came and my husband and I were ready to embark on the wonderful, scary world of parenthood, things didn't go according to plan. Nothing was happening. Time passed. I waited. I went to see doctor after doctor. Months passed and I was finally diagnosed with endometriosis and was booked in for a laparoscopy to remove what they told me was likely to be a 'mild' case of endometriosis. When I came round from the anaesthetic after my op I asked to speak to my surgeon as nobody had come to speak to me about how the operation had gone. The nurse went to get him and I heard him say "oh her" outside of the safety of my curtain. My heart sank. It was something about his tone. It wasn't going to be good news. He came in. "You have severe endometriosis so we couldn't remove it. You are likely to need IVF". BANG! This hit me like a truck. I was alone in my bed in a busy ward with people to my left and right and had just been told something that could change my imagined path of life forever. I cried quietly, conscious of the other people around me. I felt numb, I felt as though somehow I was a failure and was letting my husband down. I mean my sister had three children, my mum had four children so what the hell was wrong with me?

After the shock of being told I would be unlikely to conceive naturally, I took action and booked a further course of laparoscopies to remove this evil endometriosis that had robbed me of my chance to conceive. I changed my diet, I bought books, I stopped drinking, my husband

and I fought. My life was completely consumed with getting pregnant. The pressure on both my husband and me was enormous. I was obsessed. I put all my energy into making this work. I saw a reflexologist and an acupuncturist regularly and I got my date for the egg transfer. When the day came I was nervous but calm. The procedure was more painful than I thought it would be but I'd have endured any amount of pain if it gave me the chance to become a mother.

I discovered about ten days later I was pregnant. Words can't describe the overwhelming feeling of delight I felt about being pregnant, yet it was tinged with fear. I was scared – not about the responsibility of being a mum but the fear of 'doing' something that might endanger this person… would it be ok to carry a bag of shopping? What about exercise? As time passed and antenatal checks were ticked off I became more relaxed and started feeling able to plan and buy things… Oh, all the things that babies 'need'! The choice was unbelievable!

When my beautiful baby girl was born, after a somewhat traumatic birth, I fell in love with her at first sight. I cried. My husband cried. The relief that she had made it safely into this world and that I had managed to keep her safe for nine months felt miraculous. I never knew love like it.

My daughter is now six years old and I have a four year old boy who was conceived naturally – oh the wonders of the human body - and I love them more than anything in the world. However, I do lose my temper with them sometimes. I get cross when I stand on a tiny bit of plastic that came out of a kinder egg, which is no good to man nor beast but has been left in the middle of the floor because it might be played with in three months time; my heart sinks when I've taken time making a nice homemade dinner for them and they push it round their plates and ask for a sandwich; I shout when they are screaming at each other in order to make myself heard and in order to get their attention. I am a mum but I am also human.

Know this new mummy, your baby will bring you absurd amounts of joy but there will be a lot of other feelings too – fear, anger, sadness, guilt and a million other emotions that I had never felt so acutely before becoming a mum. But know that you're human, that you're doing an amazing job and your baby/little person in your life knows that you love them more than life itself (even if you do shout occasionally!)

Love J ♡

DO keep your identify

Dear Mummy,

How to offer advice on the biggest challenge you will ever face? A moment that will change not only your everyday life forever but you, as a woman, as an individual, for the rest of your life! I can only share my story....

Having your first baby is a daunting but nonetheless amazing experience, whether your birth story is traumatic or idyllic, it kicks off a journey which is the rollercoaster ride of your life. This brand new human whose life is quite literally in your hands, the sense of responsibility inevitably weighs heavily upon your shoulders.

You will probably spend the next year or so, bundle in tow, over copious cups of tea with other new mothers, vying to voice that birth story, empathising with varying tales of trauma from all angles. Couple that with daily rounds of sleep trumps, the winner being who gets the least - you get the idea, we all fall into a pattern of relentlessly oversharing, as we struggle with the juggle.

First time around, I relished the long days of gurgles, snuggles and unconditional love. Deliciously up to my eyeballs in baby massage, baby yoga – you name it! - we lunched, we strolled in our Mamas & Papas finest, and took in the beauty of this brave new world together, inextricably linked for eternity.

Fast forward to baby number two and I was in utter turmoil as I wasn't sure my heart had enough love to share. Two stitches and a plethora of paperwork and he was out in the world, I nailed it, Mother Earth, mum of boys - official. Soon though, it proved to be more of a challenge than I thought I had in me.

This baby boy was troubled with eczema, a milk intolerance and what seemed like the dreaded colic. He cried, relentlessly. I went through more emotions than I ever thought possible. Despair, helplessness, worry, frustration, resentment, anger. Even a tiny miracle of life you would kill for can seem like your nemesis after endless nights of sleep deprivation. I felt I was failing him, and his brother, as a mother. He was so innocent, so eager to please, and I couldn't validate his perfection, no matter how hard I tried.

Dealing with a high maintenance human, through no fault of its own, brings a massive dent in your sense of self, as you become totally immersed in the problem, turning into a worry wort, a problem fixer and an over thinker if you are anything like me.

The best advice I can give you is to remember that you are enough for you, for your baby and for the rest of your family. I totally lost sight of that.

A wearier, crankier me emerged. A moody and overburdened mum who felt the weight of two worlds on her shoulders became my norm and I failed miserably at maintaining the status quo. I could no longer find my joy, even though it was in my arms. Convinced I wasn't checking any boxes for anyone, I lurched into a spiral of self-doubt.

It took a frank exchange of views where my husband had to be very vocal and alert me that I probably needed some independent guidance for me to realise how little of me actually remained at that point. It galvanised me into making that dreaded appointment where you check the boxes that will define your future but luckily the love of my family pinpointed it at a time that a little listening, love and understanding could sort me right out.

With a great ear and expert guidance to get me to open up about my feelings, I saw, for the first time, in a very long time, that I was the lynchpin in the family, a core creator and as vital as anyone could be.

Working with my CBT counsellor, I regained a long lost sense of purpose. I actually was one of the lucky ones who was sent on the path back to finding peace with myself.

I am blessed, I am privileged, I am in awe of these wondrous children but today I am an independent woman, not just their mum. My career has become my alter ego, for better or worse, as for me, it represents life outside my mothering skills even though my everything is my babies, I still have me. Talking saved my sanity. Please don't soldier through the toughest test of inner strength you will ever face on your own. Everybody needs somebody they say and it's true.

Love with all your heart, live with your every breath, but whatever you do, don't forget the girl you once were.

Love Amanda

DO be yourself

Dear Mama

These early days may seem long, but it is so true that the years go quick. The best thing I would advise is to be mindful of the moments as they come and go. Take pauses in your day to really be present with all the little things that happen. Allow yourself to tune into all your senses. The sounds your baby makes while feeding.....the smell of your baby......look at the detail of your little love; the shape of their ears, size of their finger nails, colour of their hair and the shades and tones within their eyes. Focus on the softness of their touch as they gently explore the shape of your face with their hands and finger tips. Its all in the connection, and allowing these mindful moments will help you to be present and in tune with your baby as they grow and change each week. It is something I still take pleasure in doing with my son.

Also, not being afraid to go against the grain. You know your baby the best, and we all know that one size does not fit all. Every family, every child, has different needs and preferences. Read books and ask for advice, but take them with a pinch of salt. Be an instinctive, responsive mama who is happy to make decisions that suit your own child and their needs.

Bond, laugh, love. Enjoy those quiet, moonlit moments in the stillness of the night. Happy wishes on this amazing journey, from mother to mother with love,

El xoxo

DO what you think is best

Dear Mummies,

Congratulations on your new bundle of joy!

When I was given my daughter for the first time, I had this over whelming emotion of love. I could not believe she was mine. I kept looking at her and could not believe that she was really here. You can never remember life without children again.

Savour every moment as they grow up so fast.

When I had my second daughter I was worried what life would be like with two children. Would I feel the same sort of love?…but yes and our family was complete.

Do what you think is the best for you and your baby.

Do not wish her life away wanting her to crawl, talk, walk.

Do not panic if your friends' babies are doing things that your baby is not; nothing is wrong, and they will all get there in their own time. We all read the books, speak to friends and worry that our children have not reached that milestone at the correct age.

Getting into a routine really worked for me, but I know this is not for everyone.

You know your baby better than anyone else. You are doing a great job.

My daughters are now sixteen and twelve. I wonder where those years have gone; it seems so long ago that I was bringing them home from hospital taking them to nursery and school. They are now young ladies that I am proud of. I feel like I have blinked and they are all grown up.

Best wishes

Trish Routley

Gifts to share

A love letter back

Dear Mum,

I'm all grown up now, I know you'd be so proud of who I've become. So much of it is down to you, so I wanted to write this letter to say thank you.

When I was little, I didn't have the words or the voice to express what I was feeling in my heart, I was too little to fully appreciate those feelings and thoughts myself - now that I am grown with children of my own, that true understanding of all that you did as a mother has emerged, and I am overwhelmed with love and gratitude for having a mother like you.

I don't know if this letter will ever reach you. I pray these words can make their way back in time, to when you first had me. A time when you might not have fully appreciated how much you were doing for me and how you have changed my life. I want nothing more than for you to realise what a wonderful mother you are, and fully appreciate the difference you are making in my life – simply by being my mum, simply by being you.

I remember as a child I'd sometimes see you tired, and sometimes I'd see you cry - I know our life wasn't perfect, but I want to tell you that didn't matter - because I always knew you loved me, that you were there for me and that you were doing the best with whatever you had in that moment. What more could I have every wanted or needed from a mother!

I remember that sometimes you would worry about me. You would worry whether I was happy, whether you were giving me enough love, time, security. If only the little child I was back then had the voice that I have now, I would have taken you in my arms and held you tight, and given you back that feeling of security and love and everything being ok, that you gave to me every day. I wish I could have made you feel just for one day, all the love, kindness and security you gave to me, without realising it.

Oh Mum, if you could see the person I have already become, you would be so proud and you'd know you don't need to worry about me so much and you don't need to be so tough on yourself. All I wanted as a child was to see you happy - when you were happy that made me happy too.

I know you often tried to protect me, shield me, from the difficult parts of life. As I got older, it was these times, as difficult as they were, that helped me to grow into the strong, confident and resilient adult I am today. I saw how you were able to handle life. Seeing your courage even when you felt scared, seeing how even grownups sometimes fell over but could pick themselves back up and carry on with their held still held high.

Now that I have children of my own, I realise the precious gifts that you gave me throughout my childhood. Gifts that are beyond priceless. You taught me about life, you showed me that anything is possible when we believe in ourselves, you showed me what the words 'determination', 'courage', 'passion', persistence', 'authenticity', 'love', 'presence' truly mean.

They say we inherit our parenting style from our own parents. Part of that is the positive elements we want to re-create and pass on to our children, and part of that is sometimes what our parents did that showed us how we want to choose to not raise our own children. I can honestly say that everything I have received, taken and learned from you as a mother has been positive, even those times you felt were the difficult ones.

You have taught me not just how to love others, but more importantly you have taught me how to love myself. You taught me that through your own example, you showed me how to create happiness rather than chase it - you showed me that I didn't need other people's permission to go after my own dreams.

You would be so proud of your grandchildren if you could see them already. I see you in them - they have that same spirit, strength of character and courage. I know they will grow into happy, confident and strong adults who will create a happy life for themselves pursuing, making a positive difference in the world pursuing their own definition of success, whatever that might be - because that is what you taught our family to do – simply by being you.

I don't know if you know, but there's a book that's been written about you and your friends. It talks about your journey, the difference you make for your children, and how together you and all your friends are raising amazing future generations. The book shares messages of motherhood and love with new mums, teaching them the wisdom of the pioneering mothers who ventured before them. I am so proud that you were one of them and that you were part of making history.

Thank you for being you, thank you for being my mother, thank you for following your heart and dreams and in doing so teaching me how to do the same. Thank you most of all, for being you!

Your loving child (from the future) xxxx
(who is now all grown up with amazing children of my own who are out there following their hearts and making

the world a better place for their children and their children's children).

Nicola Huelin - author of The Invisible Revolution, founder of Mpower for mum in business

Pay it forward

How to write a love letter to a new mother;

1. Choose some beautiful paper or card.

2. Find an inspiring spot to write and put on your favourite music, maybe light a candle.

3. Tune in to all the emotions you have/had as a new mother. Be honest and don't be afraid to write everything down. Release it all.

4. Read the letter out loud. Reflect on all you have written.

5. Seal it with love, a blessing and positive vibes.

6. Send it to a new mother or leave it somewhere where a new mother might find it.

7. Know that in vulnerability comes strength, not only for yourself but for others.

About this book

This book has been lovingly created by Blossom & Berry Baby Massage & Yoga. We support mother and baby health and wellbeing by providing nurturing care for mothers and babies through our training courses, classes and services. We teach the benefits of touch, massage and yoga to help create connected and loving relationships between parents and babies to enable children to reach their full potential. Our network of teachers across the world are here to help support maternal and infant mental health through our work.

Blossom & Berry believe that love creates love. Giving love to others starts with giving love to yourself. As you nurture, value and love yourself your capacity to love and nurture others increases.

As your baby's first teacher, you can teach love, empathy and compassion by meeting your needs and those of your baby. As your baby learns the world is a loving and accepting place, he/she will develop knowing he/she is safe and secure and will grow in confidence, interacting with others with love....and so it continues; love creates love.

If we teach love to our children, there is the real possibly of a more connected society where we are accepted without judgment and we can all reach our full potential without fear.

All this love starts with you. Never forget how amazing you are; you have created another life. You are a teacher, a guide and your baby's entire universe. Mothering is unconditional love in action. Thank you for being a love creator.

"If you want to bring peace and happiness to the whole world, go home and love your family"

- Mother Theresa

"Humanity has forgotten a few very basic things; for example, touching and its tremendous importance in your life. If the mother has not taken you close to her body, to her warmth, you will remain cold your whole life; you will not be able to give love and warmth to any woman, because you never received any. You don't know that anything like that even exists"

-Osho

Useful Links

https://apni.org

Association for Post Natal Illness

http://www.pandasfoundation.org.uk

Pre and Post natal depression and other mental illness advice and support

https://www.mind.org.uk

Mental Health advice and support

https://www.bacp.co.uk

British Association for Counselling and Psychotherapy

https://www.bestbeginnings.org.uk/out-of-the-blue

Series of films promoting mental health for parents and their children

https://www.cry-sis.org.uk

Support for parents with babies who cry excessively or have sleeping problems

https://www.samaritans.org

Provides a confidential listening service

https://www.relate.org.uk

Relationship advice and support as well as counselling

https://www.womensaid.org.uk

Provides information and support for women and children and children experiencing domestic violence and abuse

https://www.gingerbread.org.uk

Support for single parents

http://ymgt.org.uk

Young mothers group trust – support for young mums

https://youngminds.org.uk

Support for children and young peoples mental health

http://www.birthtraumaassociation.org.uk

Support for people traumatised by childbirth

http://www.bliss.org.uk

Support for premature and sick babies

https://www.tamba.org.uk

Support for families with twins, triplets and more

https://www.tommys.org

Funds research into and support for miscarriage, stillbirth and premature birth and provides pregnancy health information to parents

https://www.miscarriageassociation.org.uk

Support for women after miscarriage

http://www.kickscount.org.uk

Advice on empowering women to monitor their babies movements

https://www.lullabytrust.org.uk

Information and support on safer sleep for babies

https://www.home-start.org.uk

Family support charity

https://contact.org.uk

Information and Support for families with disabled children

https://www.breastfeedingnetwork.org.uk

Support and information for breastfeeding mothers

https://www.laleche.org.uk/

Breastfeeding support

http://www.babywearing.co.uk

Information on baby wearing (use of slings and carriers)

https://www.facebook.com/groups/736604816393306/about/

Blossom and Berry Nurture Nest

www.blossomandberry.com

Baby Massage & Yoga Training, resources and information.

Notes & thoughts on your mothering journey

Record any thoughts that arise from reading this book.

Thank you & acknowledgments

A huge thank you to all the mothers who have taken part in this book. Your wisdom and love has filled this pages and gives this book power;

Jade Assowe
Aarti Bagha
Gayle Berry
Jo Coldwell
Mel Craven
Lauren Dunlop
Zoe Dury
Sandra Fernandez Conde
Amanda Fulton
Claire Holness
Nicola Huelin
Sarah Hunt
Rebecca Jepson
Helen Joyce
Emma Khangaroot
Charmaine King
Zita Lewis
Kathryn Marshall
Elaine McMahon Dossett
Colette Millar Bruce
Emma O'Brien
Becky Palmer
Jenny Parkes
Nicola Rae-Wickham
Jessica Rothenberg
Trish Routley
Carly Sherborne
Sareena Sinda
Penny Sibthorp
Josette Sticher

Sophie Thompson
Tamzin West
Susan Yeates
Jen Quinton Zorn
Jessica Scrivener

Thank you to the special team of people who helped put this book together; Jo Coldwell, Jolyon Berry & Carly Sherborne.

The profits of this book will be donated to the charity PANDAS Foundation (registered charity no 1149485) and to Blossom & Berry's charitable project in Malawi with Love Support Unite (registered charity number 1162406) which supports vulnerable mums and babies in poverty in Malawi through baby massage, safe motherhood education & health initiatives. For more details visit;

http://www.pandasfoundation.org.uk

http://www.lovesupportunite.org

https://www.blossomandberry.com/charity/little-blossom-project-malawi/

"The universe is our mother & our mother is the universe"

- Gayle Berry

9 781789 551617